A COMPLETE GUIDE TO CROSS-STITCHING

The Cross-stitch Studio

DAVID COLVIN

First published in Great Britain in 1994 by
Chancellor Press
an imprint of Reed Consumer Books Limited
Michelin House, 81 Fulham Road
London SW3 6RB
and Auckland, Melbourne, Singapore and Toronto

Production Controller: Victoria Merrington
Executive Editor: Judith More
Art Director: Jacqui Small

Produced, edited and designed by Blackjacks Ltd, London
Photography: Mark Gatehouse
Consultant and Editor: Eleanor Van Zandt
Colour Origination: Scanners

This product is suitable for ages 14 years upwards.
We recommend that children under the age of 14 years should be supervised by an adult.

Not suitable for children under 36 months.

ISBN 1 85152 650 1
Printed and bound in China
Produced by Mandarin Offset

Contents

INTRODUCTION 4

A BRIEF HISTORY 6

MATERIALS AND TECHNIQUES
Fabric 7
Threads 9
Working the Design 11
Using a Hoop 11
Needles 11
Stitches 12
Finishing Techniques 13

HOW TO DESIGN YOUR OWN CHART 14

PROJECTS
Pincushion 18
Spectacles Case 22
Card 26
Table Mat 30
Buttons 34
Napkin 38
Pillowcase 42
Alphabet Chart 46

Introduction

The decoration of cloth is almost as old as weaving itself. Embroidery, literally meaning 'work on the edge' from the Old French 'broderie', started life as a purely practical means of stopping the raw edges of woven cloth from fraying away. As time progressed, the decorative possibilities began to take precedence over more practical considerations and so the art of embroidery, as we know it, was born.

We begin this book with a section which introduces you to the basic equipment needed for cross-stitch embroidery. Unlike some forms of needlework, cross-stitch does not require any expensive equipment. The main body of the book contains seven projects for you to do. We have tried to choose objects and designs which combine beauty with practicality and which will provide you with the necessary skills and patterns to start designing things for yourself. Each project has an introduction which will give you a basic idea of the traditions and history both of the object and of the design. These sections also suggest areas in which you could do research for yourself for future designs.

In addition to the projects, there are other patterns which you will find useful when you go on to make up your own pieces. It cannot be stressed enough that there are no hard and fast rules in embroidery. Do not feel that you have to stick rigidly to the patterns and colours we have suggested; embroidery, like all forms of art, is best when it shows the individual tastes of its creator. At the back of the book is an alphabet you can use to personalize your embroidery and sheets of graph paper to help you to make your own designs.

Before you start work on any project, always map out the shape of your design on graph paper. Although it takes a little longer, the rewards are enormous. If you do not, you may find that the fabric you have is not large enough to fit the design, or that you have made some basic error in designing the pattern which cannot be corrected without removing all the stitches.

A Brief History

Examples of cross-stitch embroidery can be found in almost every decorative tradition across the world. From Mongolia to India, to South America, it has been the basic form of stitched decoration. Fragments of embroidered cloth have been found in the Egyptian pyramids; we also know that Chinese and Japanese styles of embroidery have remained virtually unchanged since the first millennium before Christ.

In Europe, embroidery was in the beginning a peasant tradition, and it was not until the thirteenth or fourteenth centuries that the upper classes started to make use of it. Peasant garments were often richly worked, both in smocking, from which cross-stitch derived its form, and in borders and figurative motifs. Even quite coarse working clothes could not escape the needle. The nobility had always relied for display purposes on damask cloths which had patterns woven into them at great cost; it was felt that embroidery was not seemly on 'great' men and women. Exactly how or why this attitude changed is not clear, but what is known is that by the end of the sixteenth century needlework skills had advanced greatly and were part of the education of every young woman.

The seventeenth century saw needlework of every kind flourishing across the class spectrum. Lace-making, an incredibly costly and time-consuming process, was rarely mastered by the ordinary needleworker, but lace patterns were widely copied and translated into other stitches. Travellers brought back from the Balkans and Bohemia examples of patterns which were quickly absorbed into the western European traditions. The primary means by which embroidery designs were recorded was the sampler. This was generally a rectangular piece of evenly woven canvas or linen worked with as many patterns, borders, alphabets and motifs as the embroiderer could remember and fit on to the fabric. The cross-stitch was the quickest, easiest and often the most beautiful way of working these various designs. Samplers were worked by every needleworker from the late sixteenth century onwards. As well as being decorative, they were also the primary method by which children learnt their alphabets until the introduction of universal education in the late nineteenth century.

In the eighteenth century there was a decline in traditional embroidery techniques. This was due to the sudden opening-up of China and Japan, which had their own very strong and distinctive decorative styles, especially in cloth, and which were much more delicate than the kind of embroidery usually seen in Europe. Eastern embroidery relied heavily on the satin-stitch, which made the fullest use of the kind of silk thread that a European needlewoman could only dream of. Oriental decorative styles swamped the native European ones, from *toile-de-Jouy* wallpaper to the Brighton Pavilion, until the dawn of the Victorian era, when there was a reverse trend back towards more traditional, home-spun styles.

Cross-stitch, in the meantime, survived by returning to its roots. When the Victorians 'rediscovered' it, the basic patterns had remained unchanged for almost a century.

Materials and Techniques

FABRIC

Cross-stitch embroidery requires a special type of fabric which is called 'even-weave' because it has the same number of 'warp' (vertical) and 'weft' (horizontal) threads per inch (2.5cm). Most of the projects in this book use a special kind of even-weave, called aida cloth, which is woven with groups of threads. Each group counts as one thread; so 14-count aida has 14 groups per inch (2.5cm).

The intersections of the groups form blocks, over which the stitches are worked. Aida cloth is available in a number of sizes, ranging from 8- count (coarse) to 18-count (fine). Single-thread even-weave is available in finer counts.

Cross-stitch can be worked on a non-even-weave or fine fabric by using a piece of embroidery canvas as a temporary grid. A special 'waste canvas', with a contrasting thread at regular intervals to make counting easier, is available for this purpose, but any non-interlock canvas can

be used. When the embroidery is finally complete, the canvas threads are removed.

Before you start working on any of the projects, you should practise your techniques on a piece of scrap cloth. While you are doing this, experiment with as many different ways of stitching as possible. For example, try using an embroidery hoop. This holds the fabric taut, preventing it from being pulled out of shape as well as making it easier to keep the stitches even. It also makes the fabric threads more visible.

One more thing before you begin work on any embroidery is to neaten the raw edges of the fabric with oversewing, using ordinary sewing thread, to stop them from fraying while you work.

THREADS

Several kinds of thread are suitable for cross-stitch. Perlé cotton is a tightly twisted 2-ply thread with a glossy, beaded appearance and is used in a single strand. It comes in several weights, or thicknesses. Soft embroidery cotton, which has a matt texture, is another single-strand thread. Stranded cotton consists of several (normally 6) fine threads, loosely twisted together, which can be used singly or combined. To use stranded thread, cut off the length that you require and separate from the skein, one by one, the number of threads you want. When working on 16-count or smaller aida, it is best to use a single strand of thread, as any more tend to look too bulky on the fine weave. Twelve- and 14-count aida are best worked using two strands of thread for the basic design. However, quite pleasing effects can be achieved by changing the number of threads you work with. For example, you

9

might lay out the basic pattern using two strands, then work areas you want to highlight in three strands, and use one strand for any area you want to look quite delicate. Ten-count or coarser cloth should always be worked with three or more strands of thread.

When you are securing threads try, as far as possible, not to knot them. While knots are undoubtedly convenient, they tend to come undone during washing and you can find that whole rows of stitching become unravelled. Instead, make several tiny backstitches in the wrong side of the fabric, which will ensure that your embroidery lasts as long as possible.

WORKING THE DESIGN

Each square on the charts represents one cross-stitch. If you are using aida cloth it also represents a single block, or intersection, of grouped fabric threads. For a single-thread even-weave, it might represent two, three or more fabric threads.

It is usually best to start working a cross-stitch design in the centre. This may be marked on the chart; or you can find it by counting the vertical and horizontal grid lines. You must also find the centre of the fabric. Measure along one side and find the halfway point; mark this with a pencil. Repeat on an adjacent side. Using a contrasting thread, work two lines of basting (long running stitch) across the centre from these two points, staying between the same two fabric threads. The point where the basting lines cross is the place to begin stitching.

USING A HOOP

While it is possible to embroider fabric held in the hand, fabric requires even tension in order for it not to loose its shape. The embroidery hoop solves this problem by holding the fabric at an even tension. A hoop consists of two rings, one inside the other. To mount the fabric, first loosen the screw on the outer ring slightly and separate the two rings. Position the fabric over the smaller ring, then push the larger ring down over it. The fabric should be very taut. If it is not, remove the outer ring, tighten the screw a little and try again. If you need to

reposition the fabric, repeat this process. However, if you must place the top ring over previously worked embroidery, first place a piece of tissue paper over the work to protect it. When the fabric is mounted, tear away the centre of the paper.

NEEDLES

For working cross-stitch you will need a tapestry needle, which has a blunt point so that it will slip between fabric threads without piercing them. This can also be used for basting, when marking the centre of the fabric. You will also need normal sharp-pointed sewing needles in various sizes for making up the article and over-sewing the canvas.

11

STITCHES

Cross-stitch

Cross-stitch can be worked in any direction. When filling an area it is best to work it in horizontal rows in two stages.

1 Work a diagonal stitch over each woven block of the aida cloth (or the chosen number of single threads) across the row (fig.1).

2 Work back in the opposite direction, crossing the original stitches (fig.2).

3 Horizontal and vertical lines of cross-stitch can be worked in this two-stage method, but when working diagonal lines you should complete each individual stitch (fig.3) before starting the next one.

Starting and Finishing

When starting or finishing a piece of work, the thread should not be secured on the back of the material with a knot because this may show through on the right side. To start, either run your new thread behind the stitches you have already worked, or hold the last 1 in. (2.5cm) of your thread behind your work and make sure it is secured by your new stitching. To finish, run your thread carefully through the backs of the stitches you have already worked (fig.5).

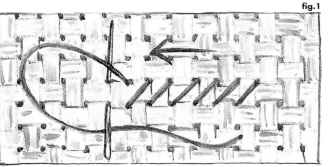

fig.1

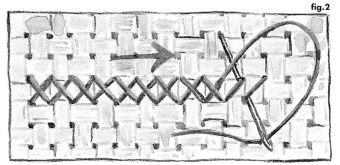

fig.2

fig.3

fig.4

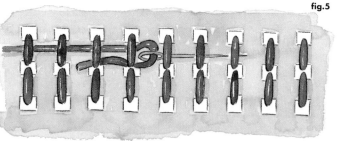

fig.5

Alternate Cross-stitch

Normally all cross-stitches within a piece of work must be formed in the same way, so that all the bottom stitches slant in one direction and all the top ones in the other. Alternate cross-stitch breaks this rule deliberately, changing the method of working here and there for a contrasting effect.

Half Cross-stitch

This is simply one half of a cross-stitch (fig.4)! These little diagonal stitches can be used to complement the square-shaped cross-stitches.

FINISHING TECHNIQUES

Oversewing

Before beginning the embroidery, it is a good idea to neaten the fabric edges to prevent them from fraying. Use a sewing needle and ordinary sewing thread for this. Fasten the thread just under the left-hand corner of the fabric. Bring the needle through to the front, then take it over the edge a little to the right, then through to the front again. Repeat. The effect is a series of diagonal stitches sloping up from left to right. The stitches can be any size you find convenient.

Turning Up a Hem

Turn under and iron the edge of the fabric to a depth just under the required hem depth. Then turn under the full hem depth and iron. Finish the hem by machine or hand.

Hand Hemming

Hand hemming is very useful for heavier fabrics, and when you do not want the hem to be too visible. Working right to left, take the needle through the hem, and then a small, catching-stitch into the main fabric.

Corners

When you are making something like the pincushion or the spectacles case, which has to be turned right-side out after stitching, you will have to cut away the corners in order to reduce bulk. Holding the fabric in one hand, cut diagonally across the corner, about 1/8 in. (3mm) away from the corner of the stitching. When you turn the item, push the corners out with a knitting needle.

Working over canvas

This technique can be used to work designs on to ready-made articles such as clothing and bed linen. Pick a canvas with the correct-size mesh for your chosen design. Cut a piece of canvas slightly larger than the design area and baste it to the fabric, making sure that the fabric is smooth and the weave aligned with that of the canvas. Work the embroidery, pulling the stitches fairly tightly. If you are using double-thread canvas, work over a single intersection of paired threads. On single-thread canvas the stitches should cross two canvas threads.

When the embroidery is complete (1) cut away any spare canvas. Dampen the work to soften the canvas threads. Using tweezers, gently pull out all the canvas threads one by one (2).

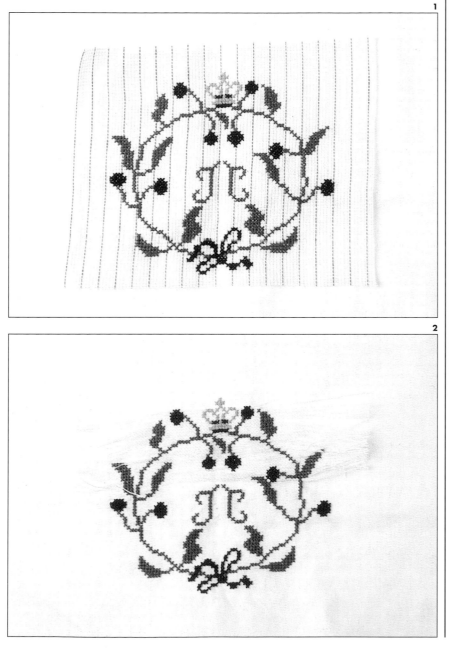

1

2

How to Design Your Own Chart

Before you begin any original piece of embroidery it is vital to put the design on paper in some form. In this way, you can get the design adjusted to your satisfaction before you begin the more time-consuming process of stitching it. In the case of cross-stitch the design is worked out in the form of a chart, on graph paper, in which each small square represents a stitch.

Charting a Design on Graph Paper

Graph paper comes in various scales and types. The most useful kind has a superimposed grid of darker lines enclosing 5 or 10 small squares in each direction. This makes counting the small squares much easier.

There are various ways of putting a design on to the graph paper. If it is a simple motif, such as a heart, you can simply draw it in pencil directly on the graph paper, adjust the outline until you are pleased with it and then go over the outline, squaring it to fit the grid. Where the shape occupies more than half the square, fill it in; where it occupies less than half, leave it blank. Once you have established the outlines of the motif, copy it on to another piece of graph paper, using either coloured pencils, or symbols to represent the thread colours.

Charting a Picture

If you wish to copy a picture from a book or magazine, the process is slightly more complex. You will need an acetate sheet marked with a grid; these are available in sets from needlecraft shops. Select a grid that will provide adequate detail for the picture. Tape the grid over the source (which can first be photocopied for convenience). This will break it up into squares. Copy the picture on to the graph paper, using the acetate grid as a guide.

Establishing the Size and Scale

Once you have charted your design, you can determine the size and/or scale of the piece of embroidery. First find the number of squares the design includes, in both directions. For example, the smaller *Pincushion* design (see page 18) contains 46 squares from top to bottom and side to side. We decided to work it on 11-count aida cloth, so we calculated the size of the fabric required as follows:

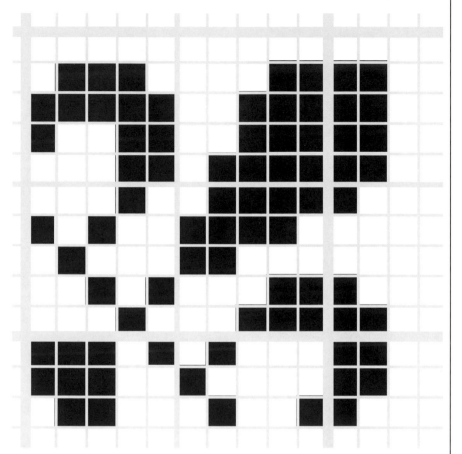

In this detail of a *fleur-de-lys* design you can see how the larger squares are sub-divided into the smaller squares and blocks.

Number of squares in design:
46x46
Actual size of embroidery on 11-count aida:
46÷11=4.2,
i.e. $4^1/5$x$4^1/5$ in. (10.6x10.6cm).

If the number of squares across and down were different the same method would be used to discover the size of both the width and the depth. Note that the measurements obtained include only the embroidered area;

add extra fabric for space around the design and for seam allowances.

Sometimes you must start with an area to be filled and then choose a suitable stitch size or fabric count (not always the same). For example, in the *Card* project (page 26) we had already decided on a window $5^1/4 \times 3^1/2$ in. (13.5x9cm). The design is 67 squares high and we needed to leave a margin above and below it – say about 16-17 squares each. Thus a total of about 100 squares must be accommodated.

We calculated the stitches per inch (2.5cm) as follows:

Number of squares (vertically) to be included: 100

Squares per inch (2.5cm):
   $100 \div 5.25$ ($5^1/4$ in.) (13.5cm) = 19.05 stitches

The closest count in aida cloth is 18-count. If we use this, the motif will measure $3^3/4$ in. (9.7cm) (67x18 = 3.72), which leaves about $1^1/2$ in. (3.8cm) space or 27 squares/stitches at top and bottom (combined) – adequate for the purpose. Double-check the suitability of this fabric for the horizontal measurement by multiplying the count (18) by the number of squares (49).

The next step is to mark out on a piece of graph paper a box containing the same number of squares as in the area to be filled (including space at the edges). Find the centre of the area by counting the squares in both directions and mark this point with a cross. Cut out the motif, leaving a one-square border round it, and place it in the box. Move it around until you are happy with its position. Pay close attention to the general balance of the whole area. The spaces between the motif and the two sides should be roughly equal, whereas the space at

For the charts in this book we have used a selction of patterns to denote the various colours used. Therefore, a key is provided with each.

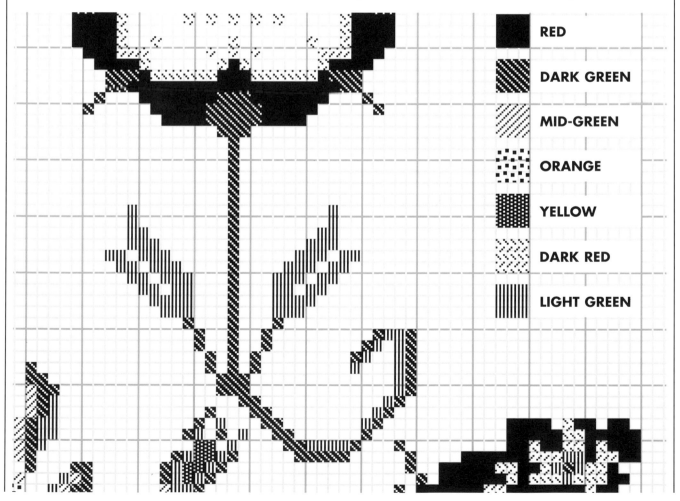

■	**RED**
▨	**DARK GREEN**
▧	**MID-GREEN**
⠿	**ORANGE**
▦	**YELLOW**
⁚	**DARK RED**
▥	**LIGHT GREEN**

the top should normally be about twice that at the bottom.

When using a printed design you may sometimes find that you wish to make it larger. This might be because you want to use a fabric with a smaller count than the one suggested, which would make the embroidery smaller than intended, or because you simply want it to be larger than the original. One way of doing this is to work four stitches for every one shown on the chart. If you are using the size of fabric specified, this will make the design twice as large as the original. Alternatively you could work each stitch over twice the number of squares in each direction. Thus, on 16-count aida you would only have eight stitches per inch (2.5cm), rather than 16. If you choose this option you will almost certainly need to use a thicker thread, otherwise the effect will look patchy and thin. If you do not want the work to be twice the size you could use a finer count aida. Similarly, you can make fine adjustments using single-thread even-weave. For example, if the design is planned for a 28-count fabric, with stitches worked, as usual, over two threads, producing 14 stitches per inch (2.5cm), you could work them over three threads to get about nine stitches per inch (2.5cm), resulting in a larger design overall. Or you could use a slightly coarser fabric and work the stitches over the two threads, as for the original.

Repeats

If you have a motif you particularly like, you might want to repeat it all over a piece of fabric. This can be done either by a random scattering of the motif or by a more formal arrangement.

Scattering: Although you may want your pattern to have a 'random' look, you will still need to plan it out beforehand. Mark several copies of the motif on to a piece of graph paper and cut them out. Then place them on a fairly large piece of graph paper and move them about until you are happy with the positioning. This will give you a guide to spacing while you are working and will ensure that you do not get odd-looking clusters on the finished piece. The more formal repeats demand a little more care but are very effective. They are based on arrangements of squares. Very small motifs can be arranged on a 10-square grid, but if you are planning anything larger you will need to draw an additional grid of the required size on to the existing grid. Use a felt-tip pen to make the large grid easily visible.

Chequerboard Repeat: Lay out one horizontal line of motifs, placing them in alternate squares. On the next line down, position the motifs again in alternating squares but this time below the squares left empty in the first row. Repeat these two rows as required. You will see that the effect resembles a chequerboard.

Half Drop Repeat: For this arrangement position the motifs in vertical rows. Begin by placing a motif in the centre of each square in the left-hand column. Then in the next column to the right, position the motifs so that they are centred on the horizontal grid lines and thus fall half-way between the motifs in the first column. Repeat these two vertical rows.

For other kinds of repeats, look at fabrics around your home, most of which will incorporate some kind of repeat pattern.

This central motif is in fact one basic design repeated eight times (four times in reverse) to make a 'snowflake' pattern.

Pincushion

Pincushions make an ideal gift for anyone who shares your enthusiasm for needlework. Traditionally they were made as tokens of friendship and love, and many beautiful examples survive from the late nineteenth and early twentieth centuries. It is still possible to find early ones in antique shops and collectors' fairs quite cheaply, and they provide a rich source of inspiration. Pincushions are a good way of using up scraps of left-over fabric, and embroidery is a particularly suitable embellishment and means of personalizing an item so intimately connected with your needlework. This pleasing geometric design was enlarged from a tiny motif in a mid-seventeenth-century sampler. A bigger motif, suitable for a larger pincushion, is also provided. You can find other appropriate motifs in books on samplers or other decorative arts.

Materials

- ❀ *Green 11-count aida cloth*

- ❀ *DMC stranded cotton in the following colours: 972 Yellow, 826 Light Blue, Blanc neige/White and 849 Red*

- ❀ *Polyester stuffing*

- ❀ *Sewing thread, needle and pins*

- ❀ *Tapestry needle size 20*

Preparation

Cut two pieces of fabric for the front and back of the pincushion. If you are making the smaller pincushion, cut the pieces 6 in. (15cm) square; if you are making the larger one, cut them 8 in. (20cm) square. If you prefer to use an embroidery hoop, cut one of the squares larger, if necessary, to fit. Oversew the edges of the top piece (the one to be embroidered) to prevent fraying. Mark the centre of this piece with lines of basting (see page 11), taking care to stay between the same two groups of fabric threads. Find the centre of the chart and mark it lightly with a pencil. Each square on the chart represents one cross-stitch taken over one woven block of fabric. The larger design measures 77 squares from top to bottom and side to side; the smaller one measures 46 squares in each direction.

Working the Design

1   First embroider the outer border in cross-stitch with the yellow thread, starting in the middle of each line and working outward, using three strands of embroidery thread. It is quite easy to lose count of the number of stitches you have worked, but it is very important in simple geometric designs like this to get it right, since one small mistake in the basic layout of the design will cause the balance of the whole piece to be lost. Now work the inside of the border and then the rows linking them, still using the yellow.

2   Using two strands of embroidery cotton, work the blue crosses at the corners, one bar at a time. Next, again using two strands, work the red and white fillings. Lastly, embroider the white bars at the corners, this time using three strands of thread.

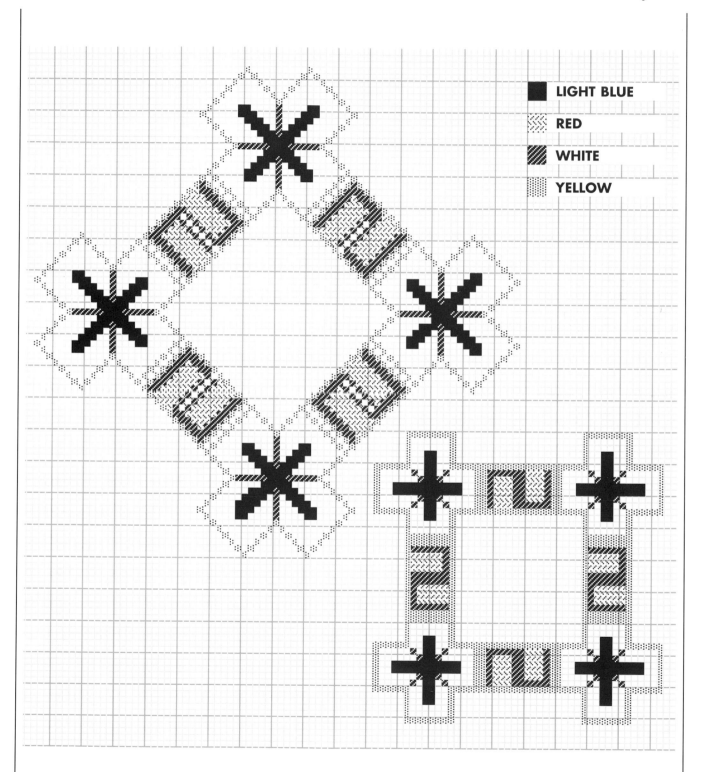

LIGHT BLUE

RED

WHITE

YELLOW

Making up the Pincushion

1 Iron the embroidery on the wrong side under a damp cloth and cut to the required size if you have not already done so.

2 Cut the other side of the pincushion to the same size as the piece you have embroidered.

3 Pin the two pieces of fabric together and stitch around the outside $^3/_8$ in. (1cm) from the edge, twice, using a short machine stitch and leaving a section about 2 in. (5cm) long unstitched along one of the sides.

4 Cut away the corners (see page 13) and turn the pincushion right side out. Push the corners out, using a knitting needle, or similar object, and fill with the polyester stuffing, taking care that it is evenly distributed around the pincushion. Close the opening with slip-stitching.

Suggestions

You could place a small motif in the centre of the pincushion. As a special personal effect, you might want to put in your own or someone else's initials. For a dressing table in a bedroom, you might prefer to make the pincushion in subtle pastel colours.

Spectacles Case

Some things simply cannot be bought in shops. It is impossible, for example, to find pretty spectacles cases, which is why we decided to make this piece. The border design came from a book on lace-work of the eighteenth and nineteenth centuries. This particular piece translated very well into cross-stitch. The embroidery in this project is worked mainly in alternate half-cross-stitch. This stitch takes a little more care and patience to embroider, but the speckled effect it gives is more than worth the effort.

particular

Preparation

1 Plan the size of your case by measuring your spectacles, then adding 2 in. (5cm) to the shorter measurement and 2^1/$_2$ in. (6cm) to the longer one which includes a seam allowance of ^{5}/$_8$ in. (1.5cm). Using a pencil or piece of taylor's chalk, mark four rectangles, side by side, on the fabric, allowing a little space between them. Cut out the four rectangles. Bind the edges of the rectangles with oversewing. If you like, mount the fabric in a hoop.

2 Next calculate how many repeats of the design you will need. Each repeat consists of six squares, and each square represents one stitch, worked over a single woven block of the fabric. Since this aida cloth has 14 squares to the inch (2.5cm), a single six-block repeat will occupy just over ^{3}/$_8$ in. (1cm). Subtract the seam allowances plus a little extra, say ^{1}/$_2$ in. (1.2cm), for the narrow margin outside the design. Then multiply the remaining distance, in inches, by the fabric count (14) to get the number of stitches in the border. Divide this number by six to get the number of repeats. If you get an uneven number, you will need to round this up or down.

Working the Design

1 On two of the rectangles mark the horizontal and vertical centre with lines of basting, taking special care to sew between the same groups of threads in both directions. Starting in the middle of each horizontal and vertical row of the design working outward, and using a single strand of light-blue thread, embroider a line of cross-stitch until you reach each edge of the design. You have now established the outermost border of the design. Next, starting in one of the corners, work a vertical line of half-cross-stitch in royal blue. Repeat this process on the other side. Do not work any of the horizontal rows yet.

2 Following the pattern closely, work the next blue vertical line of stitches in alternate cross-stitch: that is to say, the stitches should now be going in the opposite direction from the ones adjacent to them. Continue this process until all the vertical lines of the border design have been worked.

3 Now work the horizontal rows of the border in the royal blue thread. This will involve changing the direction of the thread at every stitch.

4 Work the internal alternate half cross-stitch borders in the different colours as shown on the chart. Start with the blue, then work the green and next the orange before returning to the blue.

5 Finally, work the innermost border in full cross-stitch.

6 Repeat the process for the other side of the case.

Materials

❂ *Red 14-count aida cloth*

❂ *DMC stranded cottons in the following colours:*
820 Royal Blue, 3345 Green and 720 Orange

❂ *Sewing thread, needle and pins*

❂ *Tapestry needle size 20*

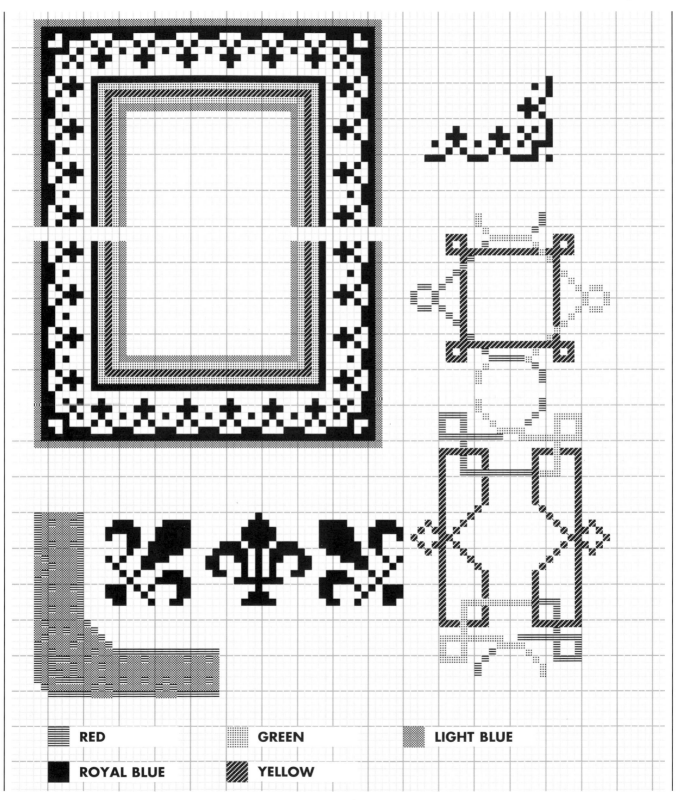

| | RED | | GREEN | | LIGHT BLUE |
| | ROYAL BLUE | | YELLOW | | |

SPECTACLES CASE

Making up the Spectacles Case

1 Lightly iron the embroidery on the wrong side under a damp cloth.

2 Cut out the four marked shapes. Place one lining piece and one embroidered piece together with the right side of the embroidery inside. Pin them together along one short edge, then stitch twice, using a short machine stitch. The double line of stitching gives extra strength. Repeat to join the other two pieces in the same way.

3 Turn both sections right side out and iron the seams. Pin them together with the embroidery on the inside. Baste along the three raw edges through all four thicknesses, a scant 5/8 in. (1.5cm) from the edge.

4 Stitch by machine, twice, just inside the line of basting. Cut off the corners and turn the spectacles case right side out. Carefully iron the seams, taking care not to crush the embroidery.

Suggestions

The open space in the middle of the design would be ideal for a monogram, worked in cross-stitch for legibility. Or you could fill it with a solid block of alternate half-cross-stitch, which gives a pleasing herringbone effect when worked over large areas.

Pergamene. 2nd cent. B.C. Laocoön

Card

The Victorians introduced the idea of greetings cards into Britain in the nineteenth century, when Prince Albert married the young queen of England and brought with him his German traditions. Embroidered cards were a very popular example of this form, and many museums have collections which you could use for inspiration. There is a strong tradition for embroidered cards in this century as well. Valentine cards are a perennial favourite and very suitable for this kind of project. The rose motif used in this project is inspired by one found on a nineteenth-century sampler. It has a very simple, rustic feel to it and illustrates how little effect two centuries of change have had on cross-stitch embroidery.

Preparing the Card

First, make sure that the surface you are working on is clean; it should also be one you do not mind cutting into (use either a special board, available from craft shops or an old piece of plywood or hardboard kept specially for this purpose). Then cut the card to size, using the craft knife. Place the card wrong side up with the long edges running horizontally. Measure in 4¹/₂ in. (11.5cm) from the left-hand edge and draw a vertical line across the card at this point. Draw another vertical line 4³/₄ in. (12cm) from the right-hand edge. Next, with the craft knife, score very lightly along the lines you have drawn and fold. In the middle of the card, you should now have a section 4³/₄ in. (12cm) wide by 7 in. (18cm) long. Draw the shape of window you require on to this section and cut it out with the craft knife.

Preparing the Fabric

Cut the fabric 6¹/₂ in. (17cm) square (or larger if necessary to fit a hoop). Oversew the fabric edges and mark

Materials

- ❋ White 18-count aida cloth

- ❋ DMC stranded cotton in the following colours: 3345 Green, 3011 Light Green, 498 Dark Red and 349 Red

- ❋ Piece of light card 7x14 in. (18x35.5cm)

- ❋ Tapestry needle size 20

- ❋ Fabric glue

- ❋ Craft knife

- ❋ Piece of hardboard for use as a cutting board

- ❋ Soft pencil

- ❋ Ruler

the centre of the fabric with basting stitches (see page 11). Find the centre of the design on the page and mark it lightly with a soft pencil. If you are using a ready-cut card bought from a craft shop and its window is not large enough to contain the rose, simply omit a few stitches from the stem. Each square on the chart represents one cross-stitch taken over one woven block. Use two threads of the stranded cotton.

Working the Design

1   Count five squares down from the centre point and start at the top of the stem. Work down the design in the dark green thread, using two strands of thread (in cross-stitch). Work the light-green leaves and the stem in alternate cross-stitch, which will catch the light in a different way and highlight the difference in the colours.

2   Work the petals of the rose in the two shades of red along one side at a time. Again, you may find it effective to work the two shades in the petal in alternate cross-stitch.

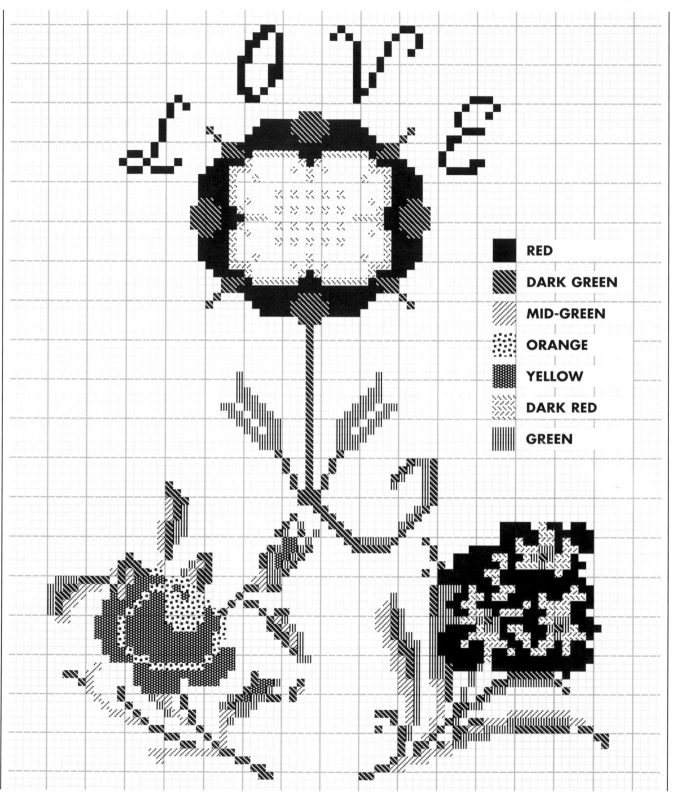

RED

DARK GREEN

MID-GREEN

ORANGE

YELLOW

DARK RED

GREEN

3 Work the leaves which show under the petals with the dark green thread.

4 Then work the middle of the rose in the dark red thread.

5 Finally, work the message in the red.

6 Remove the basting stitches.

Making up the Card

1 Iron the embroidery lightly on the wrong side under a damp cloth.

2 Trim the fabric edges to leave a rectangle measuring $6^1/2$ in. (17cm) high and $4^1/2$ in. (11cm) wide, taking care to trim evenly so that the design is still centred.

3 Place the card wrong side up. Apply a thin layer of glue around the inside of the card window and very carefully stick the embroidery in the window. Apply another thin layer of glue to the inside of the left-hand section of the card and stick to the back of the embroidery.

Suggestions

You could use any sort of design for this project. You might like to use a Christmas tree, or a decorated egg for Easter, or a bunch of flowers or a figurative scene for other occasions such as Mother's day or weddings. You could also use the card in a landscape (horizontal) format, rather than an upright one, which would also mean that you would be able to fit a longer message into the design. If you want a different message on the card, make sure you have fully worked out on graph paper the size of your window and the positioning of the letters before you start; there must be enough room for them in the window and they must also be equal spacing between them.

Table Mat

The border design used in this project was inspired by eighteenth-century trellis-work. Borders like this and the other examples shown opposite are a wonderful way of trimming plain fabrics around the home, from dresses and skirts to table and bed linen. There are literally hundreds of different styles of cross-stitch flower borders, from very strong, formal ones which in the past tend to be used on heavy fabrics like candlewick and corduroy, and lighter, more whimsical designs which are more often found on silk and linen antique pieces. Using a coloured cloth is a very good way of creating a bold impression. We thought that the red of this fabric would look very good against the rich wood of our table, and the green leaves are very striking against their complementary red. Included on the chart are other border designs you might prefer to use.

Measuring Up

What size of table mat you make is your choice. The size we used was 9x12 in. (23x30cm), but the best thing to do would be to measure the diameter of the largest plates you use and add 2 in. (5 cm) at the top and 4 in. (10cm) at the sides, plus an extra 3/4 in. (2cm) all round for the hem allowance.

Preparation

Cut a piece of the fabric about 2 in. (5cm) larger on the left, top and bottom edges than the unhemmed size of the mat, or large enough to fit a hoop, if used. This is to give yourself some extra fabric around the area you will be embroidering. Oversew all the edges to prevent fraying. Mark the left-hand edge of the position for the embroidery with a line of basting. Also mark the top and bottom finished edges at this point with two short lines of basting. You can either work the embroidery from top to bottom edge or position it so

Materials

- ❀ Red 14-count aida cloth

- ❀ DMC stranded cottons in the following colours: 3345 Green, 820 Royal Blue, 826 Light Blue, 972 Yellow/Gold, 743 Light Yellow

- ❀ Tapestry needle size 20

- ❀ Sewing needle, thread and pins

- ❀ Embroidery hoop

that it ends a few fabric threads in from these edges. Each square on the chart represents one cross-stitch worked over one woven block of the fabric. Each repeat covers 12 woven blocks, or about 7/8 in. (2cm). Measure the fabric to determine the number of repeats you will need and the best way to position them.

Working the Design

1 Starting at the bottom, first work the green leaves and stem all the way to the top. This will help to establish the vertical pattern, making it easier to position the flowers, and will save you having to change the colour of thread you are using. Use two strands of the thread.

2 Work the flowers on the right of the stem, one colour at a time.

3 Work the little flowers on the left of the stem, one colour at a time.

4 Remove the basting stitches.

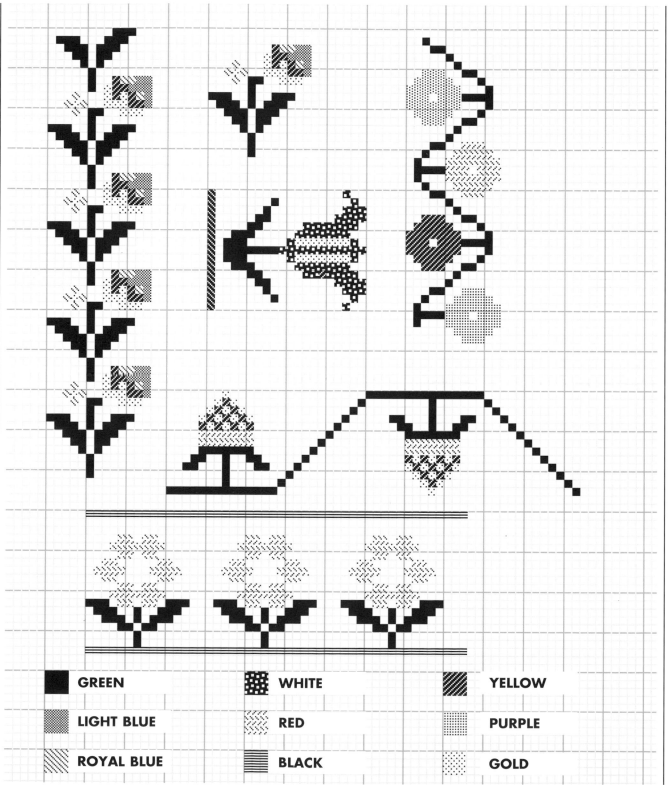

GREEN

WHITE

YELLOW

LIGHT BLUE

RED

PURPLE

ROYAL BLUE

BLACK

GOLD

Making up the Table Mat

1   Lightly iron the embroidery on the wrong side under a damp cloth. Cut the table mat to the required size, if you have not already done so, remembering to include the hem allowance.

2   Turn up the hem, mitring the corners as follows. Iron under the entire $3/4$ in. (2cm) hem allowance, taking care to include the same number of fabric threads on each edge. Now iron under each corner diagonally at the point where adjacent crease lines cross. The raw edges of the corner should be aligned with those of the main fabric. Trim off the corner $1/4$ in. (5mm) in from the diagonal fold to reduce bulk. Turn under a scant $3/8$ in. (1cm) on all edges and iron. Then re-fold along the original crease. Baste this double hem in place.

3 Sew the hem in place by hand, slipstitching the edge of the mitred corners to hold them firmly together.

Suggestions

Ideas for borders are easy to work out and can be sourced from fabric or wallpaper pattern books. Embroidery on a white background can take on a completely different look when worked on a coloured cloth.

Instead of hemming the table mat, you could fringe it. Simply machine stitch around the edges, leaving the chosen allowances for the fringe. Then pull out the warp/weft threads on each edge up to the stitching and iron. When working a horizontal border, use a design such as the roses or the lilies shown in the charts on page 31.

Buttons

We tend to think of buttons as being an integral part of the clothing of every age. However, until the Middle Ages and even after, clothes were fastened either with hooks and eyes or with decorated pins and clasps. The covering of pieces of stones with cloth introduced a new form of decoration into clothing.

Nowadays, covered buttons are an excellent way of using odd scraps of fabric and thread and are a very colourful way to add personal details to what might otherwise be quite plain clothes. When choosing your buttons, make sure that the design you want to use will fit on the button itself. We used 7/8 in. (2.2cm) moulds in order to be able to use the figurative motifs, but if you are using smaller buttons, it is better to stick to geometric patterns.

Materials

- 14-count aida cloth in various colours

- 7/8in. (2.2cm) button moulds

- Pair of compasses

- Sewing needle and thread

- DMC stranded cottons in the following colours:
  972 Yellow, 349 Red,
  810 Black, 729 Brown

- Fusible interfacing

Preparation

Using a compass or a round object of the required size, draw a paper template of a circle twice the diameter of the button mould. For example, to cover a button 7/8 in. (2.2cm) in diameter, you will need a circle 1 3/4 in. (4.4cm) in diameter. Cut out the template and use it to draw the required number of circles on the fabric. For ease of working, do not cut out the fabric circles until you have finished embroidering the motifs.

Working the Embroidery

Find the centre of one circle (counting fabric threads if necessary) and mark it temporarily with a pin. Find the centre of the motif. Each square on the chart represents one cross-stitch, worked over one block of woven fabric. Begin working the motif, starting at the centre point and using one strand of the embroidery thread, or, if you prefer, two strands.

Making up the Buttons

1   Cut a piece of fusible interfacing large enough to back all the marked circles. Iron it to the wrong side of the fabric, using a hot iron. The interfacing will ensure that the fabric does not fray while you are making up the buttons.

2   Sew a line of tiny running-stitches just inside the circle you have drawn on the cloth, leaving about 1in. (2.5 cm) of loose thread at each end. Do not secure the running-stitch,

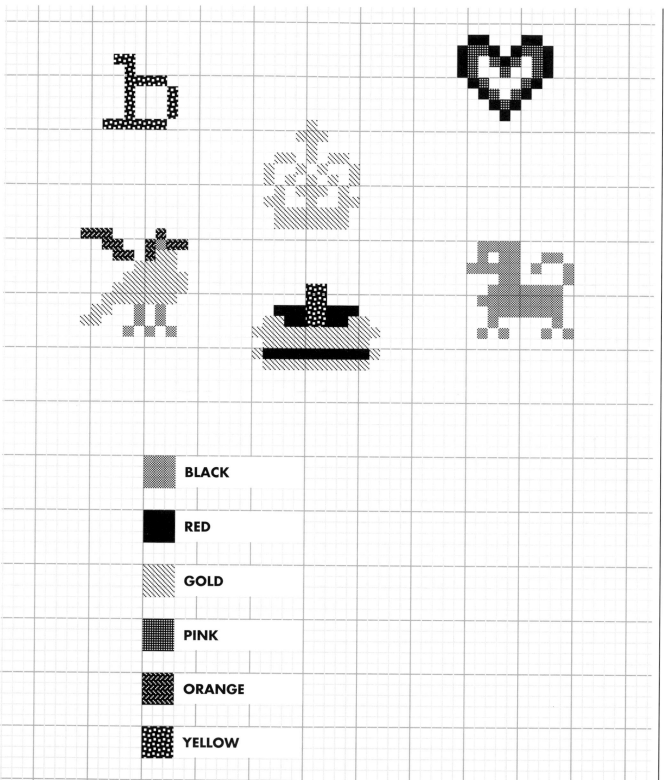

	BLACK
	RED
	GOLD
	PINK
	ORANGE
	YELLOW

BUTTONS

as you will need to be able to pull it to tighten the covering later.

3 Cut the cloth just outside the running-stitch.

4 Place the button mould in the middle of the covering and, taking hold of the two loose threads, pull the covering tight around it, making sure that the button mould itself is in the exact centre of the covering.

5 Place the covered mould face down and push the back section over it, enclosing the raw edges. Press very firmly so that it clicks into place. If you have trouble, remove the back and push the fabric edges well down into the mould, using a pointed object such as a knitting needle, and try again. It is most important that the back fits securely so that there is no chance of the button coming apart in use. Trim off the sewing thread ends.

Suggestions

Covered buttons are a very simple and effective way of using embroidery in your everyday life. Plan the motifs you want to use before you start. If you want a more complicated design, then use a fabric with a finer count. We used a 14-count fabric, which made available only about 11 blocks to embroider on using the size of button we wanted. If you use an 18-count aida fabric and the same size of button, you would have approximately 18 blocks. Small motifs like the ones shown on page 35 are easy to design and look very distinctive when placed on your favourite pieces of clothing. Textile museums are usually a good source of inspiration for motifs like these.

Napkin

Embroidered napkins always lend a touch of class and elegance to the table, especially if they are made of fine linen. It can be quite difficult to find high-quality damasks and linens nowadays, but patient searching can be rewarding. The Irish still weave the finest cloths of these types and their trade authorities will probably have suggestions as to where to look. Large pieces of embroidery often tend to obscure the qualities of the fabrics on which they are worked, and we felt that we did not want to swamp this very fine damask with a massive and involved design. The weeping willow and urn pattern used in this project is all the more striking for its simplicity. It was used in many early nineteenth-century samplers as a corner motif. You could use napkins you have, but it is very easy to make new ones yourself.

Materials

❀ *Piece of fine linen or damask or ready-made napkin*

❀ *Ten gauge double-thread canvas*

❀ *DMC stranded cotton in the following colours: 310 Black, 3345 Green*

❀ *Crewel needle size 7*

❀ *Sewing needle, thread and pins*

❀ *Pair of tweezers*

Preparation

Check the size of the linen or damask you are using. A lot of fine fabrics come in widths of 36 in. (90cm), so that one length would make four napkins measuring 18 in. (45cm) square. Cut the fabric to the desired size and hem by hand or machine, mitring the corners (see page 33). Fold the napkin in quarters and choose the best position for the motif. Mark the position of the bottom right-hand corner of the motif with a small cross in the sewing thread. The motif is 28 squares high and 20 wide. Each square on the chart represents one cross-stitch taken over one intersection of paired canvas threads. Cut a piece of canvas about 3x4 in. (7x10cm). Pin it to the napkin with the lower right-hand corner overlapping the cross by about 1/2 in. (1.5cm), taking care to align the grains of the two fabrics. Baste the canvas in place about three threads from the edges and diagonally from corner to corner to prevent the napkin

from slipping while you work. Do not secure the basting stitches too firmly. Remove the pins.

Working the Design

1   Remove the marked cross from the linen.

2   Begin working the design in cross-stitch at the bottom right-hand corner of the design, first working up the willow and then moving to the ground and the urn. Use a single strand of thread in the needle. Since napkins generally receive quite heavy wear through frequent washing, make sure that you have firmly secured the embroidery threads on the wrong side of the linen, at the beginning and end of the stitching. Take care as you embroider not to sew through the canvas threads.

3   When you have finished stitching the design, remove the basting stitches. Holding the linen in

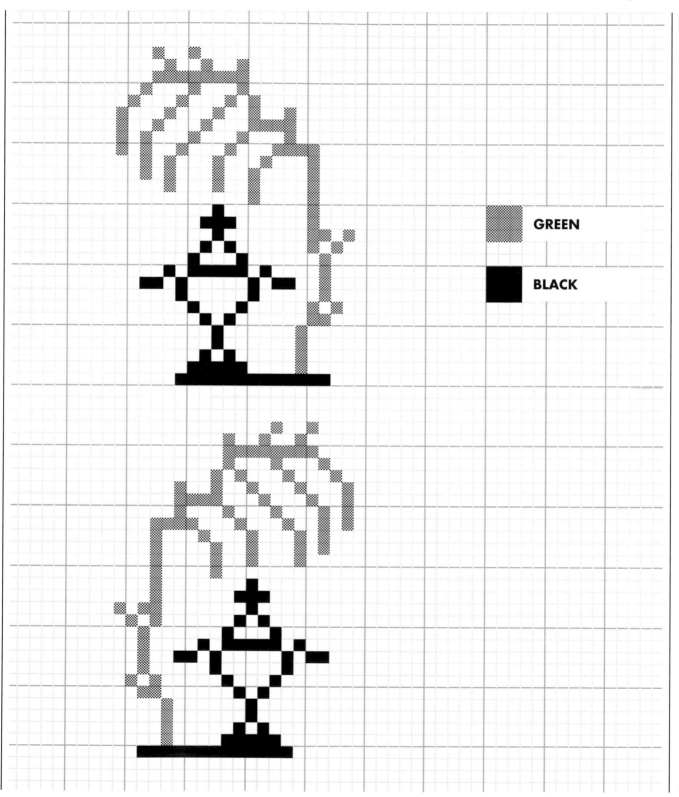

GREEN

BLACK

NAPKIN

one hand, take hold of the topmost
horizontal thread of the canvas in a
pair of tweezers and very gently pull,
easing the thread through the
embroidery. Repeat the process until
you have removed all the horizontal
threads and then, by the same method,
remove all the vertical threads. If, by
any chance, you have sewn through
any of the canvas, there are two
methods for dealing with the problem.
Either, using a small pair of
needlework scissors, cut the canvas as
close to the offending stitch as possible.
Or, if the embroidery is too solid,
immerse the whole piece of embroidery
in lukewarm water and gently ease
the canvas thread from the mesh
while still wet. Whatever you do,
never jeopardize the embroidery by
pulling too hard on the threads.

Suggestions

You could decorate other fine pieces
of linen or silk with this motif. It
would also look very pretty, for
example, on a matching tablecloth,
with one urn placed in each corner.
On a large tablecloth, you would
probably find it best to make the
design larger. To enlarge a cross-
stitch motif you can transfer it on to
another piece of graph paper, marking
in 4 squares for every single square in
the original. Or use one of the other
methods described on page 15. This
motif could also be worked on a fine
single-thread even-weave fabric,
(which comes in 45 in. (140cm)
widths, suitable for small tablecloths)
without using the canvas.

Pillowcase

Pillowcases are a beautiful finishing touch to any bedroom. Although a lot of bed linen was traditionally worked in white thread, we preferred to use a selection of vivid colours for this design. The holly wreath was inspired by an early nineteenth-century motif. Patterns such as this have largely been forgotten in favour of more geometric ones but, as with some of the other projects, the resurgence of interest in traditional designs has inspired us to look to the past. A monogram is optional, but does add a nice personal touch.

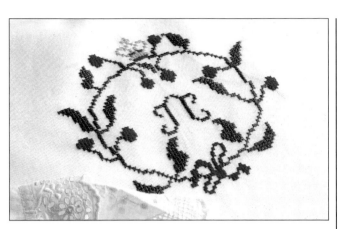

Preparation

You could make your own pillowcase, but considering the good quality and price of ready-made ones, you might as well buy one from a shop. Fold the pillowcase in half lengthways and iron using a hot setting along the fold. Do the same along the width. Baste along both creases using the sewing thread. The design measures 62 squares in height and 78 in width; each square on the chart represents one cross-stitch. Cut a piece of canvas 5¹/₄x5³/₄ in. (13.5x14.5cm) and mark the centre with a washable pencil. Do not use an ordinary pen or pencil, as it might stain the work when the canvas is dampened and removed. Place the canvas over the fabric with the longer measurement running horizontally and pin it in place, aligning the centre marks and matching the grains of the two fabrics. Baste it to the fabric, two or three threads from the edge, from corner to corner diagonally, from top to bottom and from left to right, to prevent the pillowcase from slipping while you work.

If you wish to add a monogram, plan it on graph paper, making the letters 12 squares high and 8 or 9 wide.

Materials

* *Pillowcase*

* *Double thread 10-gauge canvas*

* *DMC stranded cotton in the following colours: 3345 Green, 349 Red and 972 Yellow/Gold*

* *Sewing needle*

* *Dark coloured sewing thread*

* *Pins*

* *Washable pencil*

* *Crewel needle size 10*

* *Pair of tweezers*

Working the Design

1   Start in the centre of the design and work the letters in cross-stitch, using one strand of embroidery thread throughout. Make sure that you secure the embroidery threads firmly on the underside of the pillowcase, so that they do not come loose in the wash. Next, work the crown in the yellow thread, and then work the ribbon in the red thread. Now work the circular wreath in the green. You should now have the basic design worked out on the fabric.

2   Work the leaves, one at a time, using a new piece of thread for each leaf. This will avoid leaving long strands of thread on the wrong side, which might subsequently break or catch and cause the embroidery to come unstitched.

3   Finally, work the berries in the red thread, again ensuring that you secure and cut each thread before you continue with the next one.

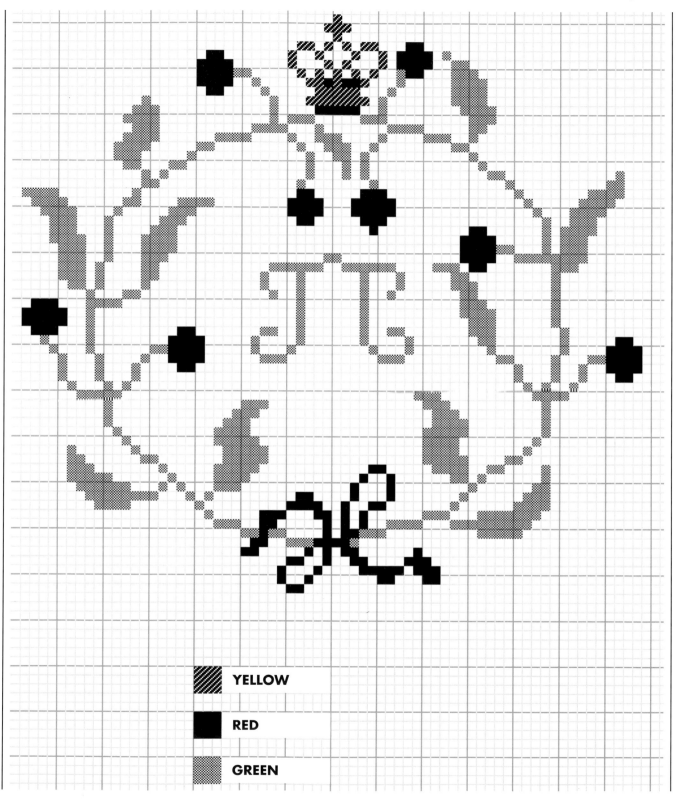

YELLOW

RED

GREEN

PILLOWCASE

Finishing the Pillowcase

1 Cut the spare canvas from the embroidery, leaving a border of about $5/8$ in. (1.5 cm) all around. Holding the pillowcase in one hand, take one of the outer vertical threads (warp) of the canvas in a pair of tweezers and pull it gently away. Repeat the process until you have removed the whole of the warp. Next, do the same with the horizontal threads (weft). There are no rules to say that you have to remove the threads in this order, so if you want to pick and choose at random, it will not effect the finished piece. If you are finding the threads difficult to remove, immerse the canvas in lukewarm water and try the process while it is still wet.

2 Iron the embroidery on the wrong side under a damp cloth.

Suggestions

This design would be well suited to being worked in white thread for a more sophisticated effect. You might also like to use it to pesonalize a dressing-gown or any other piece of clothing for a special present.

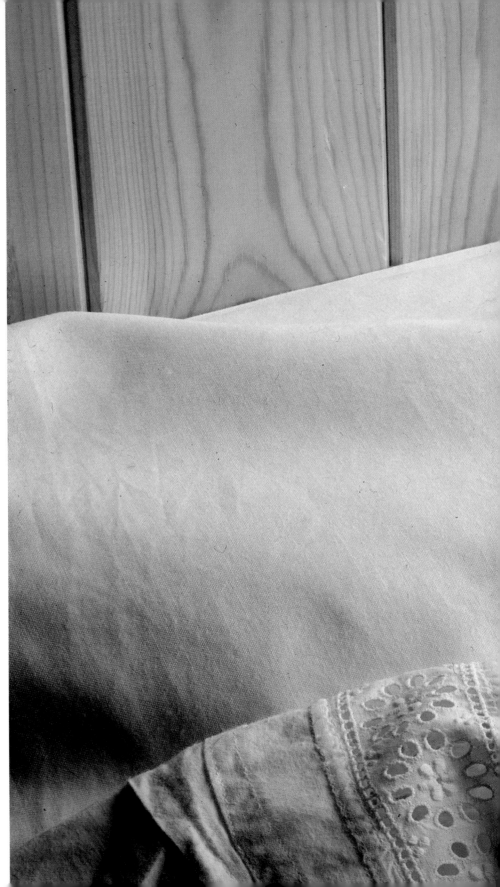

Alphabet Chart

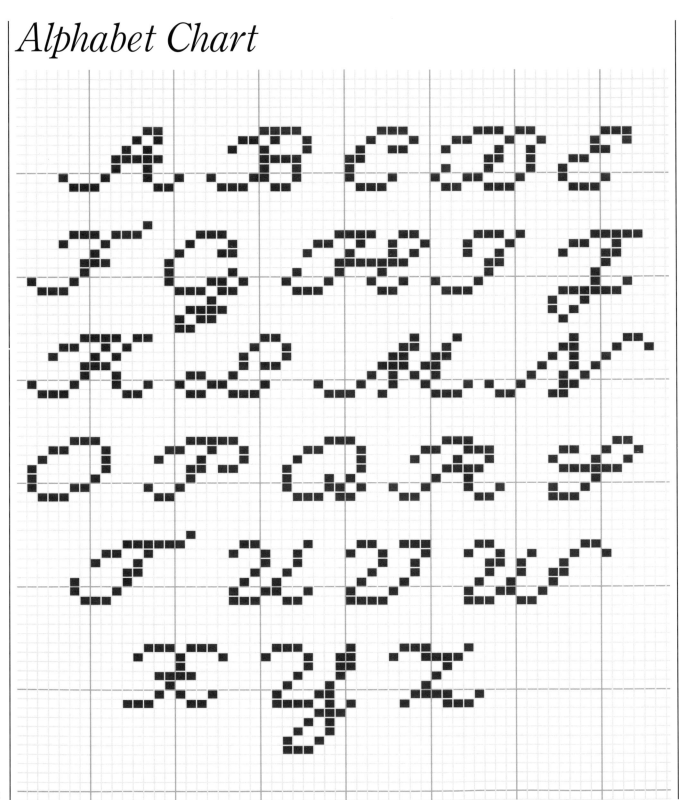

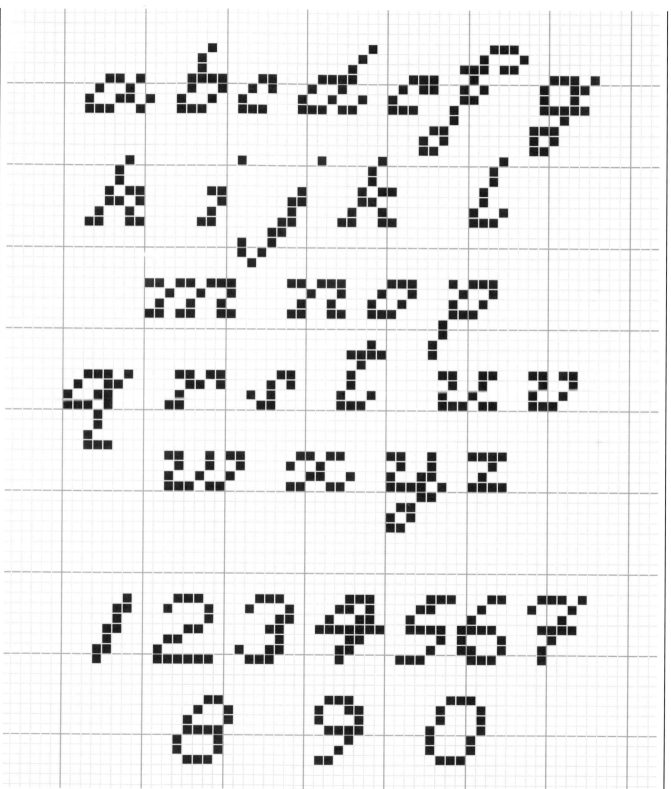